Is New York The Best City in The World?

Jamie James

CONTENTS

FIRST – IS NYC THE BEST CITY?

F*ck Yes!

There's a 100% chance that I'm going to say yes to that one

Do fish swim?

Yes, yes, and yes!

Undoubtedly!

Certainly

Yuppers

Give me a 'y.' give me an 'e.' give me an 's.' give me a 'yes!'

Heck Yeah!

Even my dog is saying yes

Do vacuum cleaners suck?

Is the pope Catholic?

No doubt

Indubitably

For sure

Indeed

Yes

Naturally

Hell Yes!

Yep

Si

Yeah!

Verily

Without a doubt

Heck Yes!

Absobloodylootely

SECOND – IS NYC THE BEST CITY?

Fo Sho

YAAAZZZZ

[nodding my head up and down]

Positively

It truly is

Yuh

Yip

Yeppers

Goddamn Yes

Is the sky blue?

A thousand times, yes!

Yup!

Totally

Abso-f*kin-lutely!

Of course!

I'll answer you with my favorite 'Y' word—Yes!

You bet

Yaaa

Unquestionably

A million times, yes!

Is one plus one equals to two?

Boo yeah!

Yea

Yah

Most assuredly

Yeet!

THIRD – IS NYC THE BEST CITY?

Oui

Yeah Baby!

Precisely

That would be Y-E-S!

Is the sun hot?

Beyond a doubt

Affirmative

Correct

How do you spell yes?

Obviously

Hell Yeah!

What's the opposite of no?

Yaaas!

Do pigeons fly?

Yiss

The answer is in the affirmative

Definitely

Absolutely

Aye

The answer is a resounding yes!

Is a duck's ass water tight?

Sure thing

Ya

Unquestionably

Is water wet?

By all means

FOURTH – IS NYC THE BEST CITY?

F*ck Yeah!

Ja

You Betcha

Obviously!

Yaas baby!

You know it

F*cking Yeah!

Did you not know already?

Precisely!

Of course, baby!

Sure f*cking thing

Beyond a doubt!

That's correct

No would be a wrong answer

Aye captain

Yes, of course

Zero doubt

You can bet on it

Absolutely!

Un-f*cking-questionably

Is the sun a star?

Even my cat is saying yes

Un-f*cking-doubtedly

The answer is a f*cking yes!

Everybody knows it

A billion times yes

ABOUT THE AUTHOR

An alum of Columbia University, Jamie James lives in New York City, and is an entrepreneur.

Hope you enjoyed this book. If you would like to comment, please post a review on Amazon. Jamie can also be reached at jamiejamesauthor@gmail.com

IS NYC THE BEST CITY?